D1560632

AMID THE CHAOS

POEMS

AMID THE CHAOS
POEMS

rENEGADE pLANETS pUBLISHING Asheville, NC
marijomoore.com

Summer 2020
© MariJo Moore
Cover Art © MariJo Moore
"Amid the Chaos" Acrylic Mixed Media on Paper 16 x 24
© MariJo Moore
"Lest We Forget" Acrylic Mixed Media on Paper 16 x 20
© MariJo Moore
"The Imperfection of Balance" Acrylic Mixed Media on Paper 18 x 24
© MariJo Moore All rights reserved.
"There is Always Hope" Acrylic Mixed Media on Paper 8 x 10

No portion of this book may be reproduced in any form
without written permission from the publisher.

ISBN: 9798652907914

Layout & Design by Kim Pitman, FireflyInx.com

Printed in the USA

Also By MariJo Moore
& rENEGADE pLANETS pUBLISHING

When Spirits Visit: A Collection of Stories by Indigenous Authors
Unraveling the Spreading Cloth of Time: Indigenous Thoughts Concerning the Universe,
Dedicated to Vine Deloria Jr (co-edited with Trace A. DeMeyer)
A Book of Spiritual Wisdom – for all days
A Book of Ceremonies and Spiritual Energies Thereof
The Boy With A Tree Growing From His Ear and Other Stories
The Diamond Doorknob
When The Dead Dream
Confessions of a Madwoman
Red Woman With Backward Eyes and Other Stories
Spirit Voices of Bones
Crow Quotes, Desert Quotes, Tree Quotes, Bear Quotes, Mystery Quotes
Crow Quotes Revisited

She is also the author of *The Cherokee Little People; The First Fire,* and *The Ice Man;*
Heinemann/Rigby Education, NH and UK; Woestijnwoorden *(Desert Words)* Bilingual
edition (Dutch/English) translated by Annemarie Sauer; Uitgeverij Kramat, Belgium; and
editor of *Genocide of the Mind: New Native Writings;* Nation Books, NYC; *Eating Fire,
Tasting Blood: Breaking the Great Silence of the American Indian Holocaust;* Thunder's
Mouth Press, NYC; *Birthed From Scorched Hearts; Women Respond to War;*
Fulcrum Publishing, CO

Quotes for *Amid the Chaos*

"MariJo Moore has done it again! Within this fabulous collection of her art and poems, she weaves us in and out of current realities stemming back to the beginning of humanity. She is led by Spirit and by everything that is good. Here, she tells a truth we need to understand for change. I will continue to read this over and over to absorb the beautiful medicine she delivers. This is a must read. What I love about this book is that it is brutally honest and at the same time puts one in a state of action and delivers hope."

-Isaac Murdoch (Manzinapkinegego'anaabe / Bombgiizhik) author of *THE TRAIL OF NENABOOZHOO and Other Creation Stories*

"*Amid the Chaos*, MariJo Moore gives voice to the concepts of foreshadowing, foreboding, and forgiveness, and to the paroxysms of anguish and anger, transcending into profound reflections, and creating for us prose and poetry born out of a kind of revulsion and love. Her painted images of formless forms, and colors, express artistic renderings of unsettled thought, and unlimited possibilities, conceived from depths of hopelessness and hope."

-Gabriel Horn (White Deer of Autumn), author of *Motherless, Spirit Drumming,* and *Ceremony*

"Rich with stunning artwork that moves fragmented turmoil towards healing, Amid the Chaos offers a portrait of psyches undergoing biological and social pandemic, a time when the Earth has been ravaged and "sneezes have become as bullets," when people working together to bridge chasmic schisms are met by bullets and other modes of murder, destruction, and death. For anyone who has been overwhelmed or unwilling to take this fully to heart, welcome to a long view: a historic view, a prophetic view. Welcome to a view from the depths, the heights, and within that can help you locate your own answers to agonizing questions: 'Which is the right prayer? Where is the love? Can humankind ever find one single thing upon which to agree? Can we deal with the ever deepening and ever ripening wounds of our psyches?'

If we face how we've harmed each other, we can find our way to heal each other: 'All of the Earth holds the memories of all ceremonies,' and MariJo Moore's poems gift us with suggestions to enact this relatedness. Culminating poems clarify that Earth is the source of the answers She loans us. May they help us all, small aspects of the Mother that we are."

- Menoukha Robin Case, co-author of _Weaving the Legacy: Remembering Paula Gunn Allen_, and _Introduction to Feminist Thought and Action: #WTF and How Did We Get Here_, and author of _Tidal River Sediment_, and _Waiting to be Special_

Introduction

This is unquestionably a challenging time in our lives. Blame abounds - going in all different directions, hitting squarely or bouncing off to be passed on to another decision maker. Even those who once stated "I have no politics, cultural or otherwise," are beginning to reconsider their choices. We are in the throes of a major global pandemic, a time of recollecting and rethinking our decisions concerning the place and purpose of humanity on the planet. Economic worries, speaking to others through panes of glass and shields of plastic, staying away from loved ones, remote learning, wearing protective gear and being mindful of all contact is not what people are accustomed to. But neither is having to put lives on the line every day - and I am referring to those in all walks of life who are "essential heroes" to whom I give my utmost admiration. But there are good things coming from this time as well: Air quality is better than it has been in a long time, people are realizing what they can do without, some are rediscovering their families, and others are becoming grateful in an unprecedented manner. Will this be an awakening to remind humans that we can take nothing on Mother Earth for granted?
For some, yes, but for others, sadly, no.

Add to this a societal pandemic - one concerning the accumulation of years of racism and inequality caused by those who are indifferent to compassion of humanity. Peaceful protesters are in the streets, demanding justice. Race baiting is prevalent, infiltrators are destroying, looting, burning properties, trying to divert the true cause of those who want to see lasting change, who want necessary policy renewal, who demand to be respected and treated as equals who want systemic poison cleansed.
This is indeed a chaotic time.

So how does poetry fit into this chaotic time?
Poetry has a way to transform raw emotions into something plausible.
A way for souls to share and maybe dispel fears, offer encouragement, give
thanks, voice disgust, tell the truth. It is a universal form of expression that
ties many together during times of crisis, of uncertainty, of questioning,
of renewal. Poems can be medicine in a Spiritual sense.

Several months ago, I began writing poems of a nature that I deem poignant,
emotive, even disturbing. I know these poems are timely and so I have
put them in this collection. I have also added some poems that were written a
while ago - some that seem even more pertinent now. I have read and reread
all and come to understand that not only do they hold much wisdom, they also
offer an invitation to rethink who we think we are as humanity.
Some of the poems are exceedingly deep, others offer revelations in a few
simple but didactic lines. Regardless, they are poems of necessity.

These, including the artwork - as are all my creations - are gifts from Spirit
that come through me. I welcome those who believe in respecting all of Earth
and all Her inhabitants to hopefully think and rethink as you explore this book.
It is somewhat of an experiential, emotional coping process for me.
Perhaps it can be of some help to others.

MariJo Moore June 2020
In the mountains of western North Carolina

To All The Ancestors

Who Live On Inside Of Us

"Amid the Chaos"
Acrylic Mixed Media on Paper 16 x 24
© MariJo Moore 3/2020

AND NOW

Sneezes have become as bullets.
Coughs as swords. Fear is palpable.
We feel it when we look at our cupboards.
We taste it when we eat our food.
We touch it when we wash our hands.

Were we warned? In many ways...

The earth is reminding us we are not in charge. We can no longer gut her,
abuse her, poison her for in doing this, we hurt everyone and everything.
We are at her mercy.
This too shall pass. This too shall pass.
But where will it go when it passes?

Will it rest on the shoulders of those who pretended to care and didn't?
In the hearts of those who lost what they felt they could not live without?
In the souls of all to hide out until once again
we become too self-important to remember how to be
grateful too idealistic to remember how to be respectful
too greedy to remember we are all connected too
afraid of losing what we could never control.
Or will it go into prophetic words to rest for a century
or two just as what we have today
did for so long...

THE TIME WHEN GRIEF GREW LEGS

It was the time when fear grew wings and terrorized the Earth.
The time when grief grew legs and walked into the homes of many.
The time when compassions morphed into prayers and prayers
morphed into pleadings. It was not an indulgent time for many but this
soon ceased to matter. Every bite of food CC took was taken with grains of
thoughts of how long will this last. He was grateful for
many things but gratitude didn't erase anger laced with helplessness.
He was thinking quite often about how so many were
leaving this realm and going into the next.

Perhaps they felt they would be of more help there than here during this time.
This time of fear growing wings and terrorizing the Earth.
This time of grief growing legs and walking into the homes of many.
His wife disagreed with his theory and debated hotly and with much disgust
how he was wrong. She stated that people were leaving
because they were getting sick and dying.
But when he asked why she thought this was happening, she only
shrugged her thin shoulders, rolled her wide eyes, and said she could not
read the mind of God or know how God played out redemption.

CC had thought long and even longer about what his wife said.
He wondered if he would be able to do more if he were called
to the clouds. He dreamed about what it would be like to be no more.
At least, to be no more here in this realm. His dreams must have been
strangely deep and viewed agreeably in the Ancestral Realm because two
weeks later he was sick and dying.
His wife prayed out loud and wailed softly and then prayed out loud some

more. CC heard her out loud prayers.
Heard her soft wails. But mostly he heard his own heart beat
growing more and more exhausted from performing in unison with heavy
breaths. And he was tired. Very, very, very tired of having to think.
His thoughts had become too heavy for his head to hold.

He was weak. And having never been a weak man he was becoming
more and more disgruntled with his inability to take care of himself.
His wife tended to him with an almost kindness.
A kindness she had not portrayed in years. This made him even more uneasy.
He decided he liked her better when she was abruptly curt.

His body began to long for the time to swallow him...
This time when fear had grown wings and was terrifying the Earth.
This time when grief had grown legs and was walking into the house of many.
He lay in his bed. Wet with sweat.
Drenched with contemplation of who might be awaiting him when he left, and
early that morning of December 12, 1918,
among the secrets of dawn as she was expanding her true colors, grief
walked into his house and greeted his wife.

CC's lips smiled as his Spirit drifted up, knowing that he had a choice.
He now had a choice of whether to help his wife or haunt her but being the
good soul he was, he decided - just as he caught a glimpse of an Ancestral
Being coming to greet him - that he would be back to help her as soon as he
could become adapted to his new surroundings.
But then again, he had plenty of time to do this because
there are no hands on the clocks of Spiritual timing.
As the Being came closer, he heard words that were not spoken but provoked

by thought: Word thoughts coming from a group of
Beings not yet in focus, words attached to a date in future Earth time...
A time when fear would grow larger wings and terrorize the Earth.
When grief would grow even longer legs and walk into the homes of many.
He could not understand these thought words fully
for he had just arrived and had not yet adjusted
to how Life actually worked in this cloudy realm.

CC could only distinguish one or two of the Spiritually thought projected
words but he knew without much doubt that he was hearing a date:
2019 or maybe 2020, and then,
a thought whisper of 2021...

The Story Within The Stories

The story of truth within the stories of lies is surfacing
my tired mind tells me so my waking dreams tell me so
my aching eyes tell me so my ringing ears tell me
the multitudes in pain must not be tempted to buy into another bag
of promised solutions tempting us to look the other way
to put strips of "goodies" over our deep wounds

and oh how deep these wounds are
carried over from generation to generation
getting wider and more infected by the moment
we must let the Ancestors know in ceremony, in prayers,
in screams we must ask Them, we must not be afraid to ask
Those who care enough and can, to listen

Those who care enough and can, to interpose, to give Their help,
Their guidance, Their permission to evolve because
the past cannot continue to uproot itself in repetition...
what is needed now now now
is paying attention not paying off

listen to what you know you know
not what you have been trained to believe
and ask the Ancestors - Those who care enough and can,
to listen, Those who care enough and can, to interpose,
to give Their help, Their guidance,
Their permission to evolve now
while the story inside the stories is surfacing...

THE CULT OF RHETORIC

It's all lies
It's all truth
It's all...

The world's depression has weighted me down,
pushed me flat to pray for answers.
We know too much, we know too much.
We don't know enough.

What is a crime to some is justice to others.
We fear too much, we fear too much.
What has happened to decency?
What has happened to equality?

They never were. They never were.
What we were told could, should be, and are.
Help us all. Punish us all. Leave us all. Give us all.
Which is the right prayer?

We cry, we wail.
We threaten, we complain.
We do nothing. We do nothing.
What is there to do?

Which is the right prayer? Which is the wrong prayer?
The prayers are becoming confused in the ether.
There is no agreement.
There is no unity.

When was there ever?
We don't know what we want. We don't ask for what we need.
We don't know what we need.
But we say we do... do we?

There is no clarity. There is no discernment.
There is only a world that turns on an axis of fear.
Where is the love that the world balances on?
Where is the love? Where is the truth? What do we trust?

We can no longer trust ourselves to trust others.
Perhaps we never did. Have mercy on us all.

AGE OLD WOUNDS

Are there wounds that have been cut so deep inside our psyches
that we have forgotten they exist or have we just found
all manner of ways to fill them?
To keep them full so that we learn to live with our shortcomings?
Convincing ourselves with fake symbols that we are
more advanced than we are?
Dare we uncover these deep and ever deepening wounds?

What would we find?
What would come flowing out - perhaps with a trickle or a gushing -
from these age old, ever deepening, ever ripening wounds?
Would we - humankind that we deem ourselves to be -
be able to exist without the darkness held tight within us by these wounds?

The painful darkness that gives us reasons to hate, to expel others of
difference, to compare our lives and minds to those whom we believe we think
we know - because we have been told and retold -
the stories of the mingling and weakening of their bloodlines?
Who are we to judge what we do not and cannot know for sure?

Why have we accepted the easy untruths instead of
searching for the hard truths?
Have we - as a so called society - created an illusion of defiant,
erroneous amnesia so that we may continue to concentrate
on differences instead of accepting similarities?
All have been wounded. All have wounded others.

Reasons notwithstanding, these are profound truths that need to be openly
discussed and considered before we can go forward.
We are all victims. We are all at fault.
It is the ever deepening, ever ripening wounds of our Ancestors
we are choosing to ignore.
These are the wounds living deep within our psyches.

All have hurt others whether it be for survival,
for love, for greed, for retaliation, out of anger,
or out of sheer fear of the unknown.
We are all carrying wounds that are a mixture of guilt and greed,
determination and madness.

How to reach reconciliation without destroying ourselves
and our descendants in the process?
Do we stop blaming?
Take responsibility for all that has happened to all in the past?
All that is happening in the present?

Can humankind ever find one single thing upon which to agree?
Could it be the beginning of something simple
like equity or something big like equality?
Or something that does not exist during this time of humanity?

Hypothetically say this sublime (see archaic definition) did come to pass.
That each one realized he or she were carrying pain that was not theirs but
which they had inherited either through blood memories or energetically,
and each and every one could reach an agreement
to stop punishing others for his or her misunderstood pain.

Say the superficial holdings were allowed to escape from
the ever deepening, ever ripening wounds so that the truths
could surface and begin to be understood.
What would we find existing beneath these wounds?
Could it be wonderful or even more devastating?
Love at its core capacity? Or hate at its?

Humanitarianism, Nirvana, Utopia or Dystopia?
Are we at a place in humanity where we could deal with
what lies beneath the ever deepening and ever ripening
wounds of our psyches?
Obviously, obviously not.

PEOPLE

*Their invisible masks suddenly made visible
walking around like outlaws coming out of lock down
afraid when they might have to hold up again
stumbling into overwhelming depths, considering the impossibility
of returning to what they thought they had
now hopefully realizing, behind their invisible masks suddenly
made visible, all are the same inside, all have the same needs,
at this moment given the opportunity to adapt
by being true humans instead of driven machines.*

"Lest We Forget"
Acrylic Mixed Media on Paper 16 x 20
© MariJo Moore 3/2020

Living Memories

The Spirits of the drums dancers, chants and songs
are what speak to our hearts and where our memories exist.

Without the Spirit-Memories
there can be no stories.

Without the stories
there can be no Blood-Memories.

Without the Blood-Memories there can be nothing.

Releasing Grief That I Have Been Carrying For Centuries

States of crying that resemble gasping
more than shedding tears
Ancestral memory or lives already lived or both

nevertheless
grief is being released soaking the air
with a dampening feeling of nothing akin
to remorse and everything akin to experience

floating on a wet heaviness trying to find a place to rest
as I say in sotto voce,
Dissolve. Disappear, detach from this environment...

speaking to those who hurt the earth
as much as to the disembodied grief
remembering Galileo Galilei's disambiguous utterance

after being forced by the church people
to recant his belief that the earth circled the sun –
Eppur si mouse – And yet it (the earth) moves...

Story Is A Woman

Story is a
woman. Not
long, not short. A
woman with body of
carved petroglyph
tongue of red memories
eyes of dark insight
ears of drummed
legends

hair of ageless ceremony falling onto
her skirt of history woven, tradition colored, many
gathered. Stranded myth beads float over her
breasts like crows float over timeless time.
Scavenging,

connecting words
old and new, told and retold
sung and shouted
whispered and chanted
reflecting mirrors in front
scraping medicines from behind.

Listen   children!
Story is   a woman.
Not long, not short,
A woman.   Respect her.

SHE TREMBLES

She trembles and the trees growl.
Catacombed mystery-lined innards
daring machinery to bite at her memories.
You shall be punished for this!

She trembles and the oceans roll
with wet-tasting morsels sweetened
with thick oily poisons.
Leave her be!

You've marked her eyes
torn her flesh, ate her intentions
and streaked her thighs.
It's not only too late - it's too demanding.

Scattering her memories once honored
now disgraced by progress.
Milking her breasts with pumps of steel
smearing her face with hardening makeup

building mounting erecting her belly
with toys she will someday destroy.
You silly foolish ones
who desire to capture the future in signs.

There is no future for you
save retribution and in - kind contributions
from those you say you represent.
She trembles and we all fall down.

ALL OF LIFE IS SACRED

She stared at the mountain until she began to see it breathe.
Until it was no longer a single, solitary rock, but a living part of the whole.
It became the arms of trees reaching up to touch the sky, the breast of
the river swelling outside itself, the mirror of all things past and all things
present. It became more than a mountain. It became everything.
A strong breeze lapped at her face.

Hard rain spat in her eyes. She could hear the heart of the Earth hammering
beneath her feet and feel the beatings all the way to her knees.
She knew the sun had begun its daily bleeding into the valleys behind her but
she could not turn around. She stood there and stared straight ahead until
there was nothing left to see. Until night swallowed all things past and all
things present. Until it had swallowed everything.

But still she couldn't cry. The pain was so deep she couldn't touch it to
name it or end it with her imagination. So deep she couldn't reach inside
and pull it out or push it inside to make it go deeper. It was real. So real
she could feel it choking itself on her innards. And so she waited, there in the
wet dark, until it had all of her. Until everything inside of her began to move.

All her memories began to remember themselves and all her dreams began to
redream themselves. Her heart hurt. Her head hurt. All of her body ached and
her eyes burned. Not because of what they saw but because of what
they were to see. And still she couldn't cry. She continued to pray into the
night and all through the next day.

She knew she would have died there that second night had the vision not come. The dark solidness opened around her as she watched the workings of Spirit manifesting before her, gifting her the answer to what seemed like month - long prayers. Sweat beaded on her forehead.
She smelled her own fear, tasted it as the beads ran down her lips.
What she saw frightened but did not surprise her.

Mighty mountains crumbled, strong rivers flowed backwards, and age - old trees uprooted themselves. People of all colors ran, screamed, begged for mercy. But Earth had had enough abuse, enough neglect.
Earth was shedding Herself of those who had no respect for Her gifts and bounties. As an irritated dog shakes fleas from its body,
Earth shook humans who irritated Her.

And then the air was still. Black and solid. The night closed around her as quickly as it had opened. As she fell to her knees, she knew what she had seen was to happen if changes were not made, if hearts were not cleansed of hatred and judgment, if respect was not remembered, if the old ways of honor were not restored, her vision would become a reality.
Earth could and would reject all.

For Earth is wise and knows that we need Her much more than She needs us.
The creeping dawn found her eyes full of water.
As she lay face down, her tears melting into the vastness beneath her tired body, she could hear the all-knowing winds whispering over and over, "What is not loved and respected will be taken away.
What humans attempt to control, eventually controls them."
And so she continued to weep.

The Earth, All Of The Earth Holds The Memories
Of All Ceremonies That Have Been Performed
And Practiced For Centuries

for the water, for the land, for the ancestors, for the people,
for the past, for the present, for the future

the earth hears your prayers, accepts your offerings
sees your ceremonies,
realizes your fears

do not fear to use your abilities to
awaken the memories and let the memories know
we need their power now
now more than we have ever dared to realize

"The Imperfection of Balance"
Acrylic Mixed Media on Paper 18 x 24
© MariJo Moore 3/2020

adoptation

WHEN YOU FEEL SCARED

dance
in any manner just dance

WHY WE DANCE

To dance is to pray.
To pray is to heal.
To heal is to give.
To give is to live.
To live is to dance...

DEMANDING CHANGE

Locked down
Held down
Pushed down
Burned down

Prepare for the rising of the dark red bird...
Youthful, upright and more vibrant than before...
Prepare for the world to begin to balance...
Know the darkness is being brought into light...

Prepare and pray
in whichever manner you choose...
Take a stand and prepare...
Out of the chaos comes change.
BELIEVE.

Solidarity In The Night

This was the night
All the people sang together.

This was the night
All the people dreamed together.

This was the night
All the people danced together.

This was the night
All the people prayed together.

This was the night all the people began to heal.

Percussion

Sleeping prophets are awakening
to the sounds of their hearts

beating a resonance in unison
with one another's longing.

MODERN DAY SPIRITUAL PRESENCE

June 7, 2020

There's much important work to be done.
Negativity is coming from the Earth - from all that
has happened to Her and Her inhabitants.
She is filtering this negative energy through the many
who are wreaking havoc in every area of life.

The way of Earth's design for an Awakening
demands this negative energy has a vehicle.
These are the people who believe they are better than others.
There are those who do not and cannot get the
true impact of what is going on
but there are many who do understand.

Multitudes of young people who have been born into
this time are being prepared to do what they have
come home to do.
Change is happening.

Olden knowledge is coming into focus again.
This has been buried for far too long.
Spirit is allowing this knowledge to come back
now to assist in the tremendous healing effort.

Those who have access to this knowledge
must comply by doing their part.
They can no longer play with ceremonies,
gifts or treasures that come to them.

Huge red globs, blobs of bright red energy
floating above the trees, above the Earth.
These are the Enlightened Ancestral Spirits Who
will take the negative energy as it rises
and dispel it into the Light.

History will repeat itself until the lessons are learned.
The Earth has had enough.
She is cleansing.
She is teaching once again.

We must pay attention. We must learn the lessons.
For our children, our grandchildren
and on and on and on...
Pray for a deeper understanding of your part
in the Spiritual Presence. Pray...

"There is Always Hope"
Acrylic Mixed Media on Paper 8 x 10
© MariJo Moore 6/2020

LOVE

About The Author

MariJo Moore (Cherokee/Irish/Dutch) is a mother/grandmother/
author/poet/artist/anthologist/seer/medium. The recipient of various literary
and publishing awards, she has authored over 20 books and presented several
art shows. She resides in the mountains of western North Carolina.
marijomoore.com

Made in the USA
Columbia, SC
13 March 2022

57397095R00024